Cracking Up

Using Natural Methods to Live with OCD

MARIA FLAHERTY

BALBOA.
PRESS
A DIVISION OF HAY HOUSE

ISBN: 978-1-4525-3630-9 (sc)
ISBN: 978-1-4525-3631-6 (e)

Balboa Press books may be ordered through booksellers or by contacting:

Balboa Press
A Division of Hay House
1663 Liberty Drive
Bloomington, IN 47403
www.balboapress.com
1-(877) 407-4847

Because of the dynamic nature of the Internet, any web addresses or links contained in this book may have changed since publication and may no longer be valid. The views expressed in this work are solely those of the author and do not necessarily reflect the views of the publisher, and the publisher hereby disclaims any responsibility for them.

The author of this book does not dispense medical advice or prescribe the use of any technique as a form of treatment for physical, emotional, or medical problems without the advice of a physician, either directly or indirectly. The intent of the author is only to offer information of a general nature to help you in your quest for emotional and spiritual well-being. In the event you use any of the information in this book for yourself, which is your constitutional right, the author and the publisher assume no responsibility for your actions.

Any people depicted in stock imagery provided by Thinkstock are models, and such images are being used for illustrative purposes only.
Certain stock imagery © Thinkstock.

Printed in the United States of America

Balboa Press rev. date: 7/22/2011

This book is dedicated to Michael, my soul mate and husband, and to my children who are my reason for living. Thank you for your unwavering love, support, and guidance. I love you all.

I would also like to thank my guardian angels and Archangels for always being with me and leading me to the right path. Thank You God for all of Your many blessings. I am eternally grateful.

Outline

PART ONE

OCD EXPLAINED

I'm not a bad person, although I fear that I used to come across as a cold person. I probably seemed distant. I've even been called aloof and a snob. Nevertheless, I wasn't. I was just protecting myself because I was scared. I have OCD, or Obsessive Compulsive Disorder. Generally, people who have OCD are thought to be weird, crazy, or even eccentric and snobbish. In reality, they are not. OCD sufferers are truly misunderstood.

OCD is thought to be caused by a chemical imbalance in the brain. This chemical imbalance makes the thoughts of people with OCD repeat over and over again. People who do not have this chemical imbalance have a thought, are able to let it go, and think nothing more of it. They dismiss what they don't like, and that's it - not an issue. OCD sufferers, as myself, have a thought, which many times is a disturbing thought of some sort, and this chemical imbalance causes the disturbing thought or image to replay itself like a broken record. So eventually, the person acts out to rid the thought, whether it's by counting, washing, or praying. The action makes the thought go away and the individual is relieved, but the result is temporary. The thought returns or a new one appears and the person acts out again, and again, and again. Eventually the act becomes a ritual and compulsive. The OCD sufferer realizes that what they're doing doesn't make sense, but they find that they can't help themselves. Often times, people don't know that they have OCD and they wonder, "what's wrong with me? Why am I like this?" They think they're crazy or weird and they're afraid, often times ashamed. So they suffer in silence.

I've read books and articles, and I've researched websites about OCD. All of it was informative and helpful, yet I still felt alone. No one really knows what it's like. No one knew what I really felt, how depressed I was, how often I used to cry. Over the years, I've met many people and through conversations with them, I was shocked to discover how many others have OCD. "How can this be?" I thought. "Why doesn't anyone talk about it?"

Only a few people have written books that share their experiences of OCD. Then I realized OCD is a very private and personal disease. My own friends and family have told me so many times "It's all in your head. Just stop it." If it were so easy, don't you think I would've stopped by now? Nobody wants OCD. Just ask anyone who has it. Ask their family members, it's not easy for them either. That's why I've decided to write this book. I would like to show that life could be easier if you decide to incorporate even a few of these natural methods into your daily routine. Maybe this book will also help those with OCD not to feel so alone or strange anymore. Moreover, maybe when others read this book they'll understand, even if only a little, that we're not crazy. That would be a nice thing. I'm not a doctor and I don't claim to be an expert on OCD. I just want to tell a story. This is a story about me, my family, and how I learned to live with OCD naturally.

I was diagnosed with OCD when I was 26 years old, but looking back, I think the OCD symptoms were around my whole life beginning in childhood. In middle school and high school, I remember washing my hands a lot and always being sure not to touch "dirty" things. People would comment on how dry my hands were. Learning about scary contagious diseases in Biology didn't help either. It was those high school years that I realized how fragile life really is.

Television was bombarding us with horrific images, such as war, diseases, and violent crimes. I guess that's about the time that I decided I would not watch the news. They had nothing nice to say and all the sadness made my stomach ache. I couldn't seem to let the "what if's" and sad feelings go. So to this day, I still prefer comedy to drama. I also remember checking windows and doors before going to bed. I had to make sure we were locked up in the house safe and sound. The thought of intruders would not allow me to sleep at night. I remember spending many nights in my sister's bed just so that I knew I wasn't alone.

It didn't get really bad until college where the stresses of good grades and the normal life challenges that a young adult faces increased. After getting married and then becoming pregnant with my first child, it all really hit the roof. Since being diagnosed, I've seen 11 psychiatrists and therapists combined, and I've gone through pretty much most medications and therapy that is available out there. After a while, I decided I didn't want to be dependent on medication for the rest of my life. So thus my journey began, which has brought me here. This book is for those out there suffering from OCD or for those who know someone suffering from OCD. Hopefully what I've gone through and what I've learned will help others like me get control over their situation, and possibly even get better. That's the ultimate goal, to get better without a lifetime of drugs and depression.

Since I want to get to the good stuff in Part Two, I won't spend a lot of time here in Part One going on and on about the scientific data collected over the years on OCD. This book is not a medical journal. It is a book about my life, my experiences with OCD, and what alternative healing practices worked for me. Therefore, this section is simply a brief synopsis about what OCD is and what the traditional medical treatments are that are currently out there. Although this section will be short and brief, I highly suggest to those new to OCD to read it so that you can get the basic knowledge concerning this disorder. It is good to get a decent understanding of something before you go out and try to fix it, right? So read on, and then we can begin the journey to your self-discovery and healing.

CHAPTER ONE ~
What Is OCD?

Obsessive Compulsive Disorder (OCD) is a type of anxiety/mental disorder. Those who have OCD typically suffer from intrusive thoughts, which are often disturbing and uncontrollable. These thoughts, or obsessions, in turn produce anxiety which is usually relieved, although momentarily, by repetitive behaviors or rituals, which one also refers to as compulsions. Because the relief of the obsessions by the compulsions is momentary, the person with OCD ends up going through cycles. These cycles can last for minutes or even up to hours at a time. Some who suffer from OCD know that this can take up a lot of their time and eventually their normal everyday lives can suffer because of this.

So for those who don't know how OCD feels, here's an example: I may say that I obsess and worry, and that fear runs rampant, but what is it like? Well, for me, and probably like many other individuals with OCD, it's basically a panic attack. You lose your breath, your heartbeat quickens and skips, your stomach is tied up in knots, and you just feel intensely stressed. Everyone goes through this once in a while, but when you have OCD, it's more than once in a while. It's more like fifty times a day (at least it was for me). So just for that alone, avoidance of certain things that triggered the anxiety was usually preferred. But that's how so many people who live with OCD become introverts - we're always hiding.

It's amazing how not very many people know what OCD is. However, one in 50 adults has OCD, and it is the fourth most common mental disorder in the United States www.news-medical. net. The numbers according to WebMD is that "OCD afflicts about 3.3 million adults and about 1 million children and adolescents in the U.S. The disorder usually first appears in childhood, adolescence, or early adulthood. It occurs about equally in men and women and affects people of all races and socioeconomic backgrounds".

People who have OCD may experience one or more symptoms. Some obsessions could include fear of dirt or germs, fear of causing harm to another person, fear of evil or "bad" thoughts, the need for order or symmetry, the need for cleanliness, fear of numbers or colors, preoccupation with religious matters, or persistent sexual thoughts. The list goes on and on, but these tend to be the most common obsessions.

Common compulsions include repetitive hand washing or bathing, checking things such as locks or switches over and over again, not touching "contaminated" objects such as door knobs or bathroom faucets, making sure items are in a specific order, counting while performing everyday tasks or even just counting steps as they walk, performing tasks a certain number of times, repeating prayers or words that help get rid of the "bad" thoughts, and extensive collecting (hoarding) of items. Again, these are the most common and there are other compulsions out there.

These symptoms can cause severe distress on a person and can take up a lot of time. Eventually, it can even become alienating to the individual who suffers from them. A lot of people may consider the OCD sufferer as psychotic or paranoid, but that often leads to the conclusion that they don't know what's going on. OCD sufferers know exactly what's going on, they're not clueless. This "knowing" is what causes such anxiety and distress in their lives, because they know something is wrong. In fact, many who have OCD learn to hide it very well. You probably know someone who has it, and hides it.

There are biological factors and environmental factors that cause OCD. Research has discovered that a neurotransmitter, serotonin, is usually low in the brains of OCD sufferers (WebMD). This imbalance is thought to be hereditary, so the chances of a person with OCD having a family member with OCD is significant. So serotonin and hereditary tendencies are biological factors. Environmental factors can include stressful situations in a person's life that can trigger OCD. This "trigger" is generally only in people who already have a biological tendency for developing OCD, or for those who already have this disorder. The environmental factors can include illness, major change in your life such as relationship issues or pregnancy or divorce, abuse, death of a loved one, anxiety attacks, or any other number of seriously stressful situations. Also, women who already have OCD may find that their symptoms increase during their pregnancy and postpartum, as it did for me.

OCD is not preventable and is considered a chronic disease. However, with proper treatment, an individual who has OCD can live a fairly normal life.

CHAPTER TWO ~
Traditional Treatments of OCD

Traditionally, OCD is treated with therapy and medication. In very severe cases, for those who do not respond to traditional therapy, electroconvulsive therapy (ECT) may be used. According to the Mayo Clinic ECT, or psychosurgery, is basically electric shock therapy that induces seizures. These seizures cause neurotransmitters in the brain to be released.

Traditional Therapy would include counseling and/or cognitive behavior therapy. Cognitive behavior therapy is a type of therapy that teaches people with OCD to confront their fears and anxieties. They do this by confronting their obsession and trying not to do their compulsion to get rid of the obsession. An example is someone who needs to wash their hands over and over again because they have a fear of germs. This person would be exposed to dirty things and told not to wash their hands for as long as possible. Eventually, the need to wash actually lessens, and the person realizes that "hey, I'm ok!" and this old way of thinking for them is put to a halt. They now have a control over this specific obsessive/compulsive way of thinking. This type of therapy is also called exposure therapy or exposure and response prevention therapy, which we will discuss again in Chapter Six.

Traditional medication therapy for OCD can regulate serotonin, there-by reducing obsessive thoughts and compulsive behaviors.

Here is a list of medications from NAMI (National Alliance on Mental Illness):

Anafranil (clomipramine): A *tricyclic antidepressant*, Anafranil has been shown to be effective in treating obsessions and compulsions. The most commonly reported side effects of this medication are dry mouth, constipation, nausea, increased appetite, weight gain, sleepiness, fatigue, tremor, dizziness, nervousness, sweating, visual changes, and sexual dysfunction. There is also a risk of seizures, thought to be dose-related. People with a history of seizures should not take this medication. Anafranil should also not be taken at the same time as a *monoamine oxidase inhibitor (MAOI)*.

Many of the antidepressant medications known as *selective serotonin reuptake inhibitors (SSRIs)* have also proven effective in treating the symptoms associated with OCD. The SSRIs most commonly prescribed for OCD are Luvox (fluvoxamine), Paxil (paroxetine), Prozac (fluoxetine), and Zoloft (sertraline).

Luvox (fluvoxamine): Common side effects of this medication include dry mouth, constipation, nausea, sleepiness, insomnia, nervousness, dizziness, headache, agitation, weakness, and delayed ejaculation.

Paxil (paroxetine): Side effects most associated with this medication include dry mouth, constipation, nausea, decreased appetite, sleepiness, insomnia, tremor, dizziness, nervousness, weakness, sweating, and sexual dysfunction.

Prozac (fluoxetine): Dry mouth, nausea, diarrhea, sleepiness, insomnia, tremor, nervousness, headache, weakness, sweating, rash, and sexual dysfunction are among the more common side effects associated with this drug.

Zoloft (sertraline): Among the side effects most commonly reported while taking Zoloft are dry mouth, nausea, diarrhea, constipation, sleepiness, insomnia, tremor, dizziness, agitation, sweating, and sexual dysfunction.

Celexa (Citalopram) Side effects may include dry mouth, nausea, or drowsiness.

SSRIs should **never** be taken at the same time as MAOIs.

For more information, go to www.NAMI.org. You can also find more on this subject at www.NIMH.nih.gov , and www.Wikipedia.org also has a lot of information on OCD.

As I've mentioned before, I've tried almost all of these medications, and then some not mentioned here, but always under the supervision of a doctor.

PART TWO

A BETTER WAY TO LIVE WITH OCD

In this section of the book, I will get to all the goodies that I've discovered while on my twelve-year long journey with OCD. Each chapter will be about one method that I used to lessen the ugliness of this disorder. I don't know if I will ever be fully healed, although I'm starting to think it's quite possible. Each of these methods worked for me. Hopefully they will work for you as well. Who knows, while on your journey, you might stumble across something else that works better for you. One good thing to remember is to always smile and laugh because laughter is the best medicine. It's good to crack up with the giggles once in a while. Whatever happens, this book is meant to help broaden your mind about OCD and how people can live better with it. May you have many blessings on your journey.

CHAPTER ONE ~

Your Guardian Angels

Finding my guardian angels was the one singular thing that got me started on my journey to self-healing. So I think it's important to tell you about that first. I was going through a really tough time in my life when I was in my early thirties. We had become broke, I experienced a miscarriage, we moved, and because of all of this stress my husband became an alcoholic. All of this happened within a 6-month period. A very stressful woman is what I became out of all of this. My son, who at the time was 7 years old, experienced a lot of stress of his own. He started doing badly in school as a result. Also, he seemed to lose control of his temper very easily. Our horrible stress was causing his stress, which caused more stress for us, and so on and so on. If left unchecked, it's very easy for stressful situations to spiral out of control. That's true for anyone, but especially for those who have OCD or for those who live with someone who has OCD.

OCD is a form of anxiety disorder, so it is very natural for extra stress in someone's life to make his or her OCD symptoms worse. For me, whenever extra stress entered my life, my symptoms just went out of control. Imagine what it must have been like for my husband and my son to watch me get worse. That kind of added stress on them caused their own anxiety to grow. So when I saw my family stressing out because of me, that just made me stress even more. Of course, it's no one's fault. Who knows where stress originates? We just have to take control and implement stress-relieving techniques.

I don't know if everyone believes in angels, but over the past few years, I've really established a firm belief in them. I think there's too much evidence in God and angels not to believe in them. You just have to open your eyes and look around. All I have to do is look at my children to know that God exists. To think that a human being can be created by two cells from two different people is just so amazingly unbelievable. Everything in the universe is perfect math and science. Just look at nature. Isn't it wonderful how a humungous tree can grow from a little nut, or that snowflakes are each unique? Have you ever really looked closely at a snowflake? It's heavenly perfect! That one single snowflake right in the palm of my hand proves to me that God exists. How can anyone think that all this "perfectness" was created by mere coincidence or accidental occurrences? Maybe coincidence or accidents do create, but by a greater design; also known as God. And if God created us, then God must have created angels. How could He not?

Have you ever felt that someone was watching out for you or helping you out in life? I have felt it before, and over time, I've become more aware of this. Sure, there are problems in life, everyone has them, but maybe they're part of our life "lessons" or "missions". And knowing that God and guardian angels are with you makes it much less lonely and stressful. Maybe bad situations in life could even be avoided just by listening to your instincts and gut feelings. These feelings, I believe, are our angels talking to us. We just have to listen.

I have had many discussions with different people concerning why we have OCD, or why anyone suffers with any number of other problems. I have been told that God created us flawed so that we would depend on Him for our salvation. I could never wrap my mind or my heart around that one. I don't believe God created our faults. If God created us in His own image, then that previous thought means that God is also flawed. I don't believe that. My God is not a flawed or selfish individual. My God is perfect. Since He created us in His own image, that means we are perfect as well. Look at a newborn baby. It's absolute perfection; clean, pure, and innocent. As the baby grows, life happens, and we **become** flawed.

Others also believe that we **choose** what problems we will struggle with before we are even born so that we may learn from them and grow. With this way of thinking, our goal in life, or mission, is to overcome these flaws and return to our perfect state, just as God had created us. To be one with God, we learn, we grow, we perfect, we return.

One night, a little over five years ago, I was searching the internet for some answers to my many questions and complaints. Suddenly, the page I happened to be looking at switched over to something completely different. I was now looking at an advertisement for Doreen Virtue's *Divine Guidance*. I looked at it for a little while, read the description, and purchased the book then and there. It was a long two weeks before that book finally arrived, but when it did, I think I must've read it all in one sitting.

Reading *Divine Guidance* got me back on track. I was introduced to my guardian angels, and my life has been so much richer and fuller ever since. Looking back at key moments in my life, I realized that they were always with me, helping me out. The same is true for the Archangels. They are always there. All you have to do is call on them. I learned to meditate, and have conversations with my guardian angels and the Archangels, and as a result, things got better. As mentioned in the first paragraph of this chapter, my family and I had some serious problems arise. By getting in touch with my spiritual side, within a five or six month period, my husband became a recovering alcoholic, my son improved in school and his temper also got better. My OCD symptoms were also so much better than it had previously been. Believe it or not, our finances also improved. Now I'm not saying that if you talk to your angels that it's like waving a magic wand. Angels do of course work miracles, but most of the time you have to listen to what they have to say to make it work.

For example, you could ask your guardian angels to help you get better concerning your OCD. Well, maybe for some it could be an instantaneous healing, but for me, I had to listen. First, my guardian angels told me to meditate more. How did they tell me? Well, for me it was a clear thought, one not muttled by obsessive thoughts. The thought was simply "you should try to meditate" - As simple as that. I also feel messages. It's hard to describe, but when I got this thought to meditate, I could feel it in my heart and in my gut that it was what I was supposed to do. You will find out soon enough how to recognize your guardian angel's messages. It just takes a little open-mindedness, patience, and practice.

Let's go back to my example of getting the message to meditate. I didn't have the first clue on how to meditate, so I just sat quietly, focused on my breathing and just fell into it. After a few times of doing this, I got better. I will discuss meditation in further detail in Chapter 2, but for now, I want to focus on guardian angels. After the guidance I got to try meditation, my guardian angels then told me to spend more time in nature. I took up gardening as a hobby, I went for long walks and hikes into the woods, and sometimes I just sat on the porch, listened to, and watched nature all around me. By doing this, I indeed got better. Perhaps I just needed fresh air to clear my head, or maybe being out in nature helped me appreciate life a little more. It went on and on like that for quite a while.

Now after five years of listening to my angels, my doctor's have reduced my medication; I no longer take three different kinds of medications. I only take one, which has also been reduced in dosage recently. Instead of talking to a therapist every week, I don't see one anymore at all. I don't need to. Instead of visiting my psychiatrist every week, then every month, then every three months, I don't go anymore at all. My psychiatrist decided I didn't need the therapy any more. I'm able to live with the OCD pretty nicely now with meditation and constant communication with my angels. Not only do I talk to my angels all the time, but I also pray all the time. After all of this meditating, I find I can easily speak with God or Jesus as well, or Spirit, if you prefer. I know, people who say they can talk to God are considered crazy - right? Well, call it God, Spirit, Creator, or whatever; it is possible to have conversations. These conversations can be very loving, friendly, and insightful conversations.

You might at this point be wondering what God sounds like. Well, to me, God is male because that's how I was raised. To someone else, God could be female. To those who are polytheistic (believing in more than one god), you could hear both male and female. Just for clarification, however, I will be calling this divine entity, or spirit as God, because as mentioned earlier that is how I was raised. As for hearing God talking to me, I specifically hear a male voice inside my head. It is not an audible voice, although I'm sure there are those out there who hear God speak to them from "outside" their heads. The voice of God inside my head is almost more like a thought than a voice, but it is definitely male and very strong, and loving. Jesus sounds like He's my best friend; also a strong and loving voice, but more gentle and modern with His vocabulary. Mother Maria has a sweet, angelic, motherly voice. The Archangels and guardian angels are male and female mixed all together; also very loving, encouraging, and helpful when the need arises.

And no, I am not schizophrenic or suffer from multiple personality disorder. Those serious illnesses need to be checked and properly maintained. I don't black out, I don't have missing time, and I'm not a "crazy" person as many have described me. I am a normal human being using my God given talents to speak to God and all that encompasses Him in the light. And the good news is that everyone has this capability. Some more-so than others, but everyone has the basics available to them. All you need to do is have an open heart and an open mind. That little voice that you sometimes hear, that's your guardian angel. So pay attention, and listen up. You'll be glad you did.

You may ask, "If there are guardian angels and Archangels, why don't they help us with everything all the time?" Well the answer to that is something simply called free will. The divine angels cannot intervene unless we ask them specifically for help or if we are in danger and need to be rescued from something that is not supposed to be happening to us. So if you want help with something, just ask. You cannot tell them how to fix it. I believe God has given His angels the knowledge and power that allows them to watch over us and help us. With this given knowledge and power, the angels know how to fix any problems before we even know the problems exist. So ask for help and sit back, and let it be.

There are four ways of receiving messages. **Clairvoyance**, where you "see" the messages with your mind's eye in the form of pictures or a movie, that are either true or symbolic. These pictures can be inside or outside your head. **Clairaudience**, where you "hear" guidance either inside or outside your head, which may or may not sound like your own voice. **Clairsentience**, where you "feel" messages as a sensation or an emotion. **Claircognizance**, where you just suddenly "know" something for a fact, and not knowing how you know (from *Divine Guidance*).

As I said before, if you sense that they want you to do something in order to fix your specific "problem" then listen and do it. I gave earlier examples of how I asked for help with healing my OCD. Hand washing is a big concern for many who have OCD. I asked for help to stop washing my hands. Although, I received messages from my angels telling me when NOT to wash my hands, it didn't really help. Then I realized that it was the urge to wash my hands that needed to be addressed. I asked for help to control the urge of hand washing and much to my surprise, I didn't feel the urge for several days. This process still needs to be addressed for me, because hand washing is a big stress reliever for me. So whenever I become really stressed, I start washing my hands. Simply asking the angels to help me not to give in to the urge usually helps. It's ok if you find that you have to repeat these requests. It can be a difficult thing to rewire your brain and to learn to listen to your higher self, but it can be done.

It's also a good idea to remind yourself regularly to listen to your angel's guidance. Even now after years of talking to the angels and asking for help, on occasion I'll be in the midst of some problem and think "Ach! Why didn't I ask my guardian angels for help with this?" Many angel experts will tell you to go through all these rituals and prayers and summoning spells to call on angels for help. That worked in the beginning, but for me, I find I don't need that anymore.

Most of the time, I just simply think, "help me". It's practically automatic. And almost as quickly as I ask, help is received. Isn't God awesome?

As I mentioned earlier in this chapter, looking back on my life, I can pinpoint distinct instances that my guardian angels helped me. I remember a time when I was about three, I choked on a marble. I was outside in the fenced garden, my infant sister was in her playpen on the patio, and my mom was inside cooking dinner. I don't know why at the age of three I decided I wanted to try to eat a marble, but apparently that's what I did. Maybe I thought it was a gumball, I don't know. But into my mouth it popped and it very quickly was stuck in my throat. I couldn't breathe, I tried to cough but wasn't able to. Tunnel vision set in and I couldn't hear anything but my own heartbeat. I distinctly remember thinking "I need help! Mommy!" Within seconds, my mom was standing in front of me. Although I couldn't hear anything, I could tell she was screaming and yelling in horror. My mom lifted me up, turned me, and swiped my mouth with her finger to get the marble out. Yes, I know that method is not considered safe, but it worked at that moment because it was supposed to. Thanks mom! I love you! I believe the angels would've had my mom save me whether I called for help or not. It was not my time to go, therefore, they would've saved me. By the way, I wasn't allowed to play with marbles for a very long time after that!

I recall another time in college when I was walking to my dorm room alone at night. This particular university had suites. Within the suites, there were separate bedrooms, a kitchen, and a common area. My suite had four bedrooms, and I was lucky enough to have a single bedroom that semester. Anyway, it was late at night and I was walking back to my building. My room was on the fourth floor. I passed two young men that I recognized. I had seen them before with one of my suitemates around campus. I noticed them staring at me, and it made me uncomfortable. They proceeded to stand up and walk up behind me as I walked by. I turned my head to see if they were following me, and they were. Their eyes looked into mine, and I knew they were not up to good things.

My building door was four doors down and I didn't know anyone who lived in the buildings leading up to mine, or I would've stopped for help, so I kept going. I quickened my step hoping it was in my imagination that they were following me. I figured if I speed up and they don't, then everything's ok. But they did speed up, so I started running. And much to my dismay, they began to run too.

At this point, I started praying like a wild woman, asking for help to get to my room as quickly as possible. I knew if I got to my room, which had a deadbolt and a telephone that I could use to call for help, I would be safe. And much to my surprise, I literally felt like I was flying up my building stairs. My feet barely touched the ground, and the guys were having a very hard time keeping up with me. I can't describe what it felt like, but it felt as if I was being pulled up from the front and pushed up from the back at the same time.

I was able to unlock the front door to my suite, fly in, and unlock my bedroom door just as I heard them coming through the front door behind me. I opened my bedroom door, went in, and turned the deadbolt immediately to lock my door. I then heard them walking past my door laughing and going into one of the other suite's bedrooms, the one belonging to the suitemate I mentioned before. I then heard more laughter, loud music, and loud noises, as was very often the case in this particular room. They liked to have parties. I felt very foolish, thinking they were just joking around with me for a fun and quick scare. So I just sat on my bed to calm myself, and as I sat there I remember thinking at how amazed I was that I was able to get up those stairs so quickly. Furthermore, I was amazed at how smoothly the locks on the front door and bedroom door opened considering how they always gave me trouble. Well, at that stage of my life, I was rediscovering God, but I didn't know anything about angels or miracles. So I just chalked up this incident to adrenaline.

An hour finally passed and I was finally relaxing, when suddenly there was a knock on my door. I asked who it was, just in case, and it was the police. Apparently, those two guys had vandalized the suitemate's room. They destroyed everything, damaged the walls, and poured bleach on the mattresses. I told them my story, and they asked why I hadn't called the police if I thought the young men were going into their room. I told them parties were a very common occurrence in that room, and I just assumed they were there for another one. They lived at the very end of the suite, so I couldn't tell if they were there or not. I just assumed they were because of the laughter and loud music.

Looking back, I should've called the police right away. I should've trusted my original instinct when I was running away from them that something was wrong, that it wasn't just a cruel joke. It hasn't been until recent years that I've realized that it was really Archangel Michael and my guardian angels taking me up those stairs and opening the locks for me. Archangel Michael is a protector, and assists those in need. Guardian angels also protect when you're in need. Moreover, I know my guardian angels were there because they're always there. I know that now.

About seven years ago, I had a major problem occur that actually was the very beginning of my belief in angels. It was in April, and my son and I had just returned home from a trip to my in-laws for Easter. My husband wasn't with us because at the time he was in the Army and was deployed. The drive from my in-laws took almost nine hours, and it was just my son (my only child at the time), our three dogs, and me.

Exactly a year before this trip, I was in a car accident that ended up giving me whiplash. I had to go through physical therapy and it got better, but sometimes, during stressful situations, the pain would come back. Well, the nine-hour drive back from our Easter vacation was stressful and tiresome, and I ended up with a really bad neck-ache. Once we got back home, I couldn't make the pain go away. Stretching, ibuprofen, and heating pads helped, but it was still bad enough that for two nights, I didn't get any sleep.

On the third day, I was, needless to say, completely and thoroughly exhausted. This neck-ache and lack of sleep had given me an enormous headache. It was terrible. So, I took more ibuprofen, I grabbed a cozy blanket, and I laid down on the couch with a heating pad on my neck, and decided to just relax for a couple of hours and watch a movie with my son. It wasn't my intention to fall asleep, but obviously, that's what happened. Well, my son at that young age of four and a half always enjoyed watching the previews and commercials before movies, so I put the VHS tape in and the counter on the VCR said 00:00.

He started watching the movie, and I lay down on the couch and quickly (and unintentionally) fell asleep. About twenty minutes later I suddenly woke up. I don't know what made me wake up, but I had the distinct feeling that something was wrong. I got so angry with myself when I realized that I had fallen asleep. I sat up to see what my son was doing, but I didn't see him anywhere. I looked at the timer on the VCR and it was at about twenty minutes, that's how I knew how long I was asleep. I called out for him, but he didn't answer, so I thought maybe he was playing with me or doing something sneaky again. As with most children at that young age, whenever he did something sneaky, he was very quiet. I got up to go look for him but didn't get very far when I suddenly heard the front door open up, and saw my son coming in. He was outside! I was furious! I always lock the door, that's the OCD in me. My son was always told never to go outside by himself, so why would he do this?

We were living on a military post on a very quiet street, so that fact was a sense of relief, but I was still horrified. Anything could have happened. So there I was standing and thinking all of this, while I'm looking at my little boy with rosy cheeks and his shoes on the wrong feet. He had dressed himself and snuck out to be with a neighborhood friend who was a little older, but always outside by himself. I quickly scooped my son up in my arms and started kissing him all over his sweet little face. When I put him down and started to scold him about what he had done, I heard a knock on the door.

I said "Now what? Who's that?" My son quickly replied, "It's the police, mommy. They want to talk to you. They followed me home. I ran all the way!" He said this with a big grin, like this was a cool thing that was happening. I had such a sick feeling in my stomach; I knew this was going to be very bad. Sure enough, it was indeed the police at the door and they asked me and my son to follow them to the military police station. The other little boy and his mother were asked to go as well. When we arrived, they put us in separate rooms and then someone came in to ask a whole bunch of questions. I was petrified. They kept looking at me as if I was the most horrible, disgusting mother who was neglecting and abusing her own child. This had never happened to me before, or since.

If these people knew me, they would've known that I loved my little boy more than anything and that my whole life revolved around him. Now I have two children, and I can easily say that they mean everything to me. Before this whole incident occurred, when it came to him playing outside, I was always out there. In fact, a lot of the time, I was the only parent out there watching a whole neighborhood of children. Sometimes, if there were other parents outside, I would let him play at their house or yard, but I would stay by the window to keep an eye on him, or every fifteen or twenty minutes I would go outside and check on him. I was always watching him.

I felt this situation I found myself in was very unfair. The one time I accidentally fell asleep, he had to sneak out. I got in trouble, but the other parents who let their kids out all the time with absolutely no one watching them were safe from the whole event that I found myself in. I admit, though, that I messed things up royally. I should have never allowed myself to fall asleep.

After questioning me, the police then proceeded to photograph me and take my fingerprints. They sent me home and told me that I would be contacted by social services very soon. I was petrified. I got home and just fell into a deep depression. There I was, all alone, and so ashamed. I explained to my son what was happening, and he was frightened as well. Never again, has he done anything sneaky or not listen to my instructions. What a rough way to learn a lesson.

So I prayed and prayed and prayed. I also got a lawyer. I know that every parent takes naps. Sure, I took naps too, but only when my son was also taking one and I knew exactly where he was. I never slept when he was awake and I certainly didn't expect him to figure out how to unlock and open the front door. It was just a bad set of circumstances. So the lawyer told me that I had nothing to worry about, that it wouldn't go anywhere. I prayed that he was right.

Soon, the social worker called me and we set up an appointment for the following week. At this point, it was the weekend and I realized that I would have three whole days to worry about this. I decided that my son and I would spend the weekend doing fun things together. I read in the newspaper that there was a psychic fair in town. I thought "Why not?", so we went. It was very interesting. I had never been to a fair like that before, and I don't particularly know why I went to this one. I suppose I was called there.

At the fair there were, of course, psychics, healers, and there were vendors that sold everything from crystals, to jewelry, to angel pins. There were books, and music, and lots of incense. It was really cool. I was having fun, but I was still very worried that my little boy would be taken away from me.

After wandering around, I came across this very nice looking lady who was doing angel card readings, so I thought I'd give it a try. She told me to ask the angels a question while she was shuffling the cards. Naturally, I asked if everything that was happening with me and my son, and the police and social workers, would work out and be ok. I asked this question silently in my head, because I was ashamed and embarrassed and I didn't want this nice lady to know what was really going on. She finished shuffling the angel cards, laid them on the table, and began my reading. It was a truly amazing experience! I don't really remember what the cards were, but what she said I would never forget. She said that I was having some troubling problems, and that the problems would indeed fizzle away, and that everything would work out. She said my son and I were safe. In addition, the part that really stood out for me was that she said Archangel Michael was with me protecting us. That was the first time I ever heard that, and the sense of calm that came over me, was amazing. She said that I could call on Archangel Michael anytime I needed him and that he would immediately be there for me. She said not to worry, that everything would be fine. Well, I have never forgotten that.

After a nice weekend filled with the fair, going out to lunch with my son, and going to church, the up-coming meeting with the social worker didn't seem so frightening anymore. Sure, I was still scared, but I still had this feeling that everything would be fine. I met with the social worker, and answered all her questions, made my statement and then she said that she didn't know why the police pursued this, because she had more pressing issues to work with. She also said that this report would go before a committee and that they would make the final decision as to what to do with this situation.

A few days went by, and after a whole lot of praying, I heard from the committee. They dropped the case, and the fingerprints and photographs from the police station were erased. There was no record or file. I of course got a stern warning that if this ever happened again, I would really be in serious trouble. I knew this would never happen again, so it was not an issue. I was relieved, and my belief in angels was born.

Ever since then, I've asked Archangel Michael to help me whenever I have real bad problems, including rough OCD episodes. It really works! If the OCD is truly bothering me, I ask for Archangel Michael to take care of it for me, I take a deep breath in, and I just feel the weight being lifted off of my shoulders as I'm breathing out. A sense of calmness comes over me, and I'm able to handle the OCD in a better way, or I can walk away from it altogether. It's wonderful. And I know that we're all safe.

About six years ago, I had another significant event involving angels. After years of trying, I finally became pregnant. However, this pregnancy only lasted about 9 weeks before it was discovered that it was a blighted ovum.

"A blighted ovum (also known as "anembryonic pregnancy") happens when a fertilized egg attaches itself to the uterine wall, but the embryo does not develop. Cells develop to form the pregnancy sac, but not the embryo itself. A blighted ovum usually occurs within the first trimester before a woman knows she is pregnant. A high level of chromosome abnormalities usually causes a woman's body to miscarry naturally. A blighted ovum is the cause of about 50% of first trimester miscarriages and is usually the result of chromosomal problems. A woman's body recognizes abnormal chromosomes in a fetus and naturally does not try to continue the pregnancy because the fetus will not develop into a normal, healthy baby. This can be caused by abnormal cell division, or poor quality sperm or egg." American Pregnancy Association.

As a result, my doctor recommended that I have a D&C performed on me. Well, the blighted ovum discovery and D&C all happened within two days. I did not have a lot of time to come to terms with what was going on and I didn't feel the real impact of all of this until I was in the prep room of the hospital. Usually in the prep room, you can have your family with you, but at this particular hospital children were not allowed in the prep area. We didn't know this and since our son came to the hospital with us, they were asked to wait in the waiting room.

So there I was, all alone; and I felt all my emotions rising to the surface. A wave of deep sadness fell over me and I can honestly say I had never felt that alone in my entire life. I couldn't hold back the tears any more, and I began to pray. I asked God to be with me and keep me safe. I asked for His love and help to overcome this situation. I asked not to be alone. Just then, I felt a presence in the room. It felt like there were two other people in the room with me, but no one was there. All of a sudden, I could feel this presence (or energy) move. One went to the left side of my head, and the other went to my right side. Then, it felt like the presence on my right side began to hold my right hand. It was warm and light and it tickled. It was magical, and beautiful, and I had never experienced anything like that in my entire life. Somehow, it made everything better, and I knew everything would be fine. The handholding lasted for almost ten minutes before a couple nurses came into the room to start asking me questions, and get me going on an IV. The hand holding ceased, but I could still feel them in the room. I could feel them with me when I was being moved to surgery. I could feel them with me as I was going under with the anesthesia. And they were with me when I woke up after the surgery.

This event got me going in the direction of self-discovery. Before this, I had thought about angels quite often, but had never physically experienced them. It was as if a light switch was turned on for me. They were so real! I knew I had at least two guardian angels with me all the time. And I had this intense longing to meet them.

That is how I first started my search for God, angels, and myself. As I mentioned earlier in the chapter, I came across Doreen Virtue's book *Divine Guidance*. I highly suggest this book; it has everything in there that you need to get started on finding your guardian angels.

You can meet your guardian angels through meditation; that's how I did it. I know both of their names, I know both are female, and I talk to them often. They are always nurturing, caring, loving. They also correct me sometimes, but never harshly. Guardian angels are not mean, or nasty. They don't get angry with you; they are not capable of getting angry. Therefore, if you experience an angry type of communication through meditation or through talk that goes on in your head, it is most likely your lower self, or the id and ego working together.

According to Sigmund Freud, the id and ego function basically to satisfy and take care of your basic drives such as food, water, sex and other basic impulses. The id is also selfish and amoral and doesn't care about anything or anyone else. The ego wants to please the id by supplying the basic impulses with results from the real world. Then there's the super-ego, which is the moral functioning part of our selves. It seeks perfection and is considered part of the conscience that aims for spiritual goals and a higher sense of morality. This super ego is usually termed as your "higher self". The id and ego combined is considered your "lower self". And this lower self is usually the mean, nasty, degrading voice that you hear in your head sometimes. The one telling you "you can't do that, you're not good enough". Don't listen to that voice. That voice is not your guardian angel. Your guardian angel's voice, or voices, is sweet and loving and always looking out for your best interests in being safe and loved and spiritual. That's what you want to listen to.

When it comes to hearing your angels talking to you, you just have to believe in yourself. You probably already hear your guardian angels talking to you sometimes and you don't even know it. That nice, little voice in your head; it could be your higher self, or it could be your guardian angels talking to you. The point is you should probably listen. I can usually tell if it's my higher self-talking to me or if it's my guardian angels. My higher self sounds like my own voice and my guardian angels sound completely different from me.

Guardian angels are like loving, caring parents who watch over you. In the next chapter, I will discuss different types of meditations that you can use to get started on discovering your guardian angels. You can also use these meditations to discover your spirit guides if you so choose. You can also find your totem animals and ascended masters and saints. You can even meet your higher self, which is also an ultimate goal. But for now, let's just focus on your guardian angels.

CHAPTER TWO ~
Meditation

I want to talk about meditation, because it seems to be probably one of the most important steps of this healing process. There are all kinds of meditations out there, but whichever way you choose, it will definitely help, simply because you get to know yourself better. It is also one of the best ways to connect with God.

There are considered to be three principles to meditation: First, you must be able to concentrate by focusing on one thing or object at a time. Second, gently bring your thoughts back to focus if they happen to wander. Third, while meditating, it's important to ignore any distracting thoughts or sensations. That's all fine and good, but I have one problem with these principles; they don't generally work for those of us with OCD!

The first principle of concentrating on one thing or object at a time can be quite difficult for those with OCD simply because although we are very good at focusing our thoughts, focusing on just ONE thing can be a challenge. The second and third principles of bringing your thoughts back into focus if they wander, and ignoring distracting thoughts or sensations, is like telling a person with OCD "don't wash your hands". Sometimes, the harder you try not to do something, the worse it makes the situation. So basically, for people with OCD, trying NOT to think about something is next to impossible.

When I first started meditating, I didn't know it at the time, but I was basically doing something called Reflective Meditation. There are many forms of meditation, which you can find at www.meditationtypes.com, but my all-time favorite has to be Reflective Meditation. This, I find, seems to be the most OCD friendly meditation. The reason for that is unlike Zen or Concentration meditations where you have to focus on one thing constantly, Reflective meditation is more contemplative. You basically focus on a certain question or thought and "reflect" on it. You'll see that through meditation, this deep relaxation and lucid thought process will really help with your OCD and with connecting to God and your angels. If you'd like more information on Reflective meditation, go to www.learnmeditationskills.com/reflective-meditation.html.

So now what? Well, I'll tell you how I started to meditate. It's always important that you have a quiet place where you can relax and not be disturbed. It's also probably a good idea not to do it lying down in bed because most likely you'll just fall asleep. Find a comfortable position, either in a chair or on the floor, light a candle or incense, and just relax. I like to light a candle and burn incense as a way of clearing the room from any negativity and asking God to be with me. At this point you can ask God, the angels, or the universe anything that you would like to know or get help with. To begin your meditation, close your eyes and inhale big, deep breaths through your nose, hold for a few seconds, and exhale through your mouth. These are cleansing breaths to help clear your mind and your heart. Remember to breathe through your belly, not your chest. Imagine all the muscles in your body becoming soft and pliable, from your feet all the way up to the top of your head, or vice versa.

If you are new to meditation, relaxing your muscles is the key. Focus on one group of muscles at a time, relaxing them as much as possible before moving on to the next. This process may take a few minutes and that's fine. Once your body is relaxed and your breathing is calm, just fall into your mind. This will eventually lead you into a deep state of relaxation and it is at this point that you can start to follow the flow of thoughts that come to you. If you want to focus on one particular thought, go for it. If other thoughts pop into your head, don't stress. Just acknowledge it and let it float away. If for some reason a particular thought stays with you, maybe you should go with that. Follow the thought and see where it takes you. Perhaps this thought will lead to a "problem" in your life that needs addressing. Visiting these "problems" while meditating very often helps me to cope with or get over that particular "problem".

Just remember to breathe and ask God or your angels to flow through your body as a warm bright light. Stay there in your thoughts for a while and know that you are communing with God. Usually at this point when I meditate, I will be lead to an answer to my question. Either I'll see pictures as an answer, or I'll hear my guardian angels or Jesus talking to me, or I'll just get a feeling of what I should do to address any question that I may have asked. If you want to ask other questions while meditating, this is a good time to do it. You may want to know more about your guardian angels, ask them anything. Try not to second-guess yourself or think too much. Just let it flow. For example, you may ask how many guardian angels you have. The very first number that pops into your head is your answer. You could do the same for their names or whether they are male or female. The list goes on and on. You could also ask to meet your spirit guides or animal totems. It's pretty much standard that whatever comes first is your actual answer. Don't force it.

The funny thing is that for me, even though I may ask a specific question before I start the meditation, sometimes I'll get an answer concerning a different question that may have been on my mind at the time. This is completely all right if it happens. Perhaps the different question or thought needed to be answered first. So be open, and be patient. And if you feel scared or nervous, just ask God to protect you and imagine yourself completely surrounded by a beautiful, warm, golden light. Know that you are protected and safe. When you are finished visiting your mind, you will know. If it's only been two minutes or as long as twenty minutes, it doesn't matter. As long as you take the quiet time to meditate, it will be for the better.

When you are finished and want to come out of your meditation, take deep breathes into your belly, imagine the light within you is flowing through your body from your head to the bottom of your feet and through to the earth. This will ground you. Open your eyes, wiggle your fingers and toes, and have a good stretch. Don't forget to thank God, or your angels for being with you. At this point, you can get up and go about your day knowing that even though you may not feel like you've accomplished anything, you truly did. The more you meditate, the better you'll get at it. Like everything else, practice makes perfect. And believe it or not, it has many excellent health benefits as well as being fun.

Meditation can help with many things concerning the stresses of OCD. Signs that stress from OCD, or just life in general, are taking hold of your body include: poor memory, distracted attention, drug or alcohol abuse, fatigue, high blood pressure, eating disorders, weak immune systems, low self-confidence, anxieties, and depression just to name a few. If you experience any of these symptoms, meditation could help.

According to the Transcendental Meditation Program (www.tm.org/benefits-brain), benefits from meditating include excellent working memory, focused attention, no substance abuse or addictions, energy and vitality, fit cardiovascular system, balanced physiology, strong immune system, improved self-confidence, feelings of safety and peace, happiness and optimism just to name a few. There really is a beneficial side to meditating. In fact, you could speak to your therapist and ask if they hold workshops on meditating for anxiety disorders. Many clinics and hospitals do offer such help. At these workshops you learn how to meditate and perhaps they even offer different kinds of meditation. The more you meditate, the quicker you discover what type of meditation works best for you.

From one of my favorite authors, Deepak Chopra, is a quote I found where he describes transcendental meditation so beautifully, that I wanted to share it with you.

"Transcendental meditation is one particular form of mantra meditation, and there are many, that allows your mind to experience progressively abstract fields of awareness, and ultimately you settle down in this space between your thoughts. The space between your thoughts is pure consciousness, and it's a field of possibilities, it's a field of creativity, it's a field of correlation. It's also a field of uncertainty, and it's a field where intention actualizes its own fulfillment. So meditation allows you to contact this field. It's very primordial, the ground state of our existence."

I've noticed in my life that when I forget to meditate or just put it off for whatever reason, my life tends to get more stressful again. So if you're stressing about something and you think you don't have time to meditate because you should spend your time on fixing whatever is stressing you, the irony is that if you opt not to meditate, it can actually cause your stressful situation to become even more stressful. Wow, I know it's a lot to consider.

Anyway, my point is this, even when you think you're too busy, you still should try to meditate. Take it from me. I've stopped meditating on several occasions because I thought, "hey, I'm ok now…I don't need this anymore" or "gosh, I don't have time for this right now" or "I'll do it later". All these reasons are valid in their own way, but you'll be sorry if you listened to any of them. Once you stop, you stop for a while. And if it's been a long while, sometimes it's hard to jump back in again. However, you must take the time to meditate. Meditation is the key. Like anything, if you don't practice, you may become rusty at what you're doing. But have no fear, once you get going again, it'll all come back to you. It's just that first step, whether you are a beginner or not, is always the hardest one. Just meditate, you'll find that it's well worth your time.

CHAPTER THREE ~
Diet and Exercise

Believe it or not, diet and exercise can affect your mental health. Everyone thinks about their physical health when it comes to diet and exercise, such as their weight, their cholesterol count, diabetes, and overall health in general. But the last thing that comes to mind is mental health. What you eat affects your moods; how you treat your body affects your moods. It's all chemical. Everybody knows that you have to eat a healthy diet and exercise to have a healthy body, but that should also include the brain. Meditation takes care of the mind. Diet and exercise takes care of the brain.

Much of the New Age community agree that a person who wants to achieve higher levels of consciousness and develop better communication skills with their guardian angels, ascended masters, or spirit guides should evolve to a completely vegetarian diet. The thought is that eating meat of any kind causes your body's energy to vibrate at a lower frequency, thereby causing you to not achieve higher levels of consciousness, etc. "Why is that?" you may ask. Well the argument there is that when an animal is killed for meat processing, it dies in fear and anxiety. That fear and anxiety causes adrenaline and other chemicals to rush the animal's body before it dies. In turn, it is thought that we absorb that fear and anxiety when the meat is ingested. It actually makes perfect sense to me, and back when I first heard about it (about five years ago) I decided

I would become a vegetarian. Handling raw meat always made me sick to my stomach anyway; I think I was always having flashbacks of dissecting some poor creature when I was majoring in biology during college. I hadn't eaten beef in about 11 years either, so this was just the last straw.

Sure enough, I was able to communicate better, and get a good grasp on my OCD symptoms, but I was also always getting sick with colds, my sleep was poor, and I gained about 30 pounds from this vegetarian way of living. It didn't matter that I was exercising. I still gained the weight. I don't think that everybody is built to be a vegetarian. So now I eat lean meats, lots of vegetables, some fruit, seeds and nuts. I also avoid all processed foods and grains of any kind. With this way of eating, I feel stronger and more energetic than ever. I've also lost 45 pounds so far. If you're interested in this way of eating, then take a look at *The Paleo Diet* by Dr. Loren Cordain. Another great book is *The Paleo Solution* by Robb Wolf. These books discuss how this lifestyle diet helps avoid cancer, diabetes, heart disease, Parkinson's, and even Alzheimer's, which apparently is a form of diabetes.

Now I'm not saying never to go vegetarian, and I'm not saying you have to eat meat or not eat meat. What I am saying is that you have to discover for yourself what works best for you in how you look, perform, and feel (physically and mentally). I still have problems with eating meat (it still grosses me out), but I know my body needs it. So what I do while I cook the meat is say a simple prayer. I ask God to cleanse the meat from any negativity and to fill it with His loving light to bless and purify it. I also thank God and the animal for its sacrifice and to once again bless the food that we are about to eat.

I have noticed that since being back on a diet with meat, that my OCD symptoms do sometimes get a little worse than when I was a vegetarian. But now that I also know of other ways to handle the OCD symptoms, it's ok. It's not so bad.

Here's a story that might help you decide one way or the other what kind of lifestyle diet you want to try. I was at a conference in

May of 2010 and had the pleasure of hearing Eldon Taylor and he told this story about his wife. Before they had children, they had decided to go vegetarian, but when she became pregnant with their first child, she constantly craved chicken. And so she ate chicken. It upset her, but she ate it. Long story short, she and baby turned out strong and healthy. When she became pregnant with their second child, she constantly craved beef. This time though she was determined to stick to her vegetarian diet. She did not eat beef. When the baby was born, it was fine, but she was diagnosed with rheumatoid arthritis within a week. Devastated, they tried to find alternative treatments and came across an experimental treatment that consisted of taking a concentrated form of, believe or not, beef. It apparently seemed to heal her of her symptoms.

So what's the point? Well, maybe the point is that if you crave something don't ignore it. I'm not talking about sex, drugs, alcohol, and junk food. I'm talking about real food. If your body needs protein in the form of meat, then eat it. Pray over it if it makes you feel better, make sure it's organic and cruelty free as best as you can, and thank God for it because a lot of people don't have the pleasure of "should I eat or shouldn't I eat" type questions.

Needless to say, I'm not a doctor or a dietitian, but I have done my research, and asked knowledgeable people many questions and you should probably do the same as well. Remember, it's your body. Only you know how your body works. Try either lifestyle diet and see for yourself which one works best for your OCD symptoms. You should stick with either diet for at least three months before making any judgments as to what works and what doesn't.

The Paleo diet does work for my family and me. I feel younger, healthier and stronger. A big part of this lifestyle diet is taking fish oil, aka omega-3 fats (n-3). Why do I take the fish oil? Well, it is a very important fat that is missing in our modern diet and the easiest way to get enough omega-3 is by taking fish oil. Our ancestors foraging way of life provided us with approximately 1:1 to 1:2, n-3/n-6 fats. Our modern diets provide us with 1:10 to 1:20. This huge gap is due to the fact that our dairy and meat is fed with grain and soy "while traditional sources of fat have given way to high n-6 fat sources like corn, soy, sunflower and similar seed oils. This is "No Bueno" as the n-6 family of fats influence (generally) pro-inflammatory products from the prostaglandin, cytokine, leukotriene and other chemical messenger families." ~ Robb Wolf. In other words, this modern diet is causing major inflammation in our bodies, which in turn causes health risks that can easily be avoided with fish oil. The Paleo diet effects are simple in that insulin secretion is reduced when taking fish oil. Liver pathology caused by consuming excessive carbs, a diet high in n-6 and grain based lectins will also be reversed when taking fish oil.

"High dose fish oil can literally be a life saver in this situation and from a purely mechanistic level considering the actions of GRP-120, we can understand why. (GRP-120 is a receptor that lies at the heart of the insulin resistance that results from increasing levels of systemic inflammation.) The relative lack of n-3 fats in our modern diet allows for a feed-forward progression of inflammation and insulin resistance. Folks who are sick (insulin resistant, inflamed, suffering autoimmunity) seem to benefit greatly from n-3 intake in the 1.0g ((EPA+DHA)/10lbs bodyweight/day. For a 200lb person that may mean as much as 20g of EPA/DHA per day." ~ Robb Wolf. I know this sounds like a lot, but remember that the n-3's reverse inflammation and any insulin resistance. Not only will you feel better, but you'll start to look and perform better too. "Biomarkers of health improve. Eventually folks can titrate down to ~.25g of n-3/10lbs BW." ~ Robb Wolf.

There has also been some talk amongst the scientific community that some of OCD may be an autoimmune disease. Although I must point out that nothing is certain and everybody seems to have a theory on the origins of OCD. There is even talk of OCD being linked to Alzheimer's disease. Again, nothing is certain. There is still much to discover.

There is fascinating evidence, however, that supplementing your diet with fish oil is important because having this "right" kind of fat in your diet has been shown also to reduce the effects of diabetes and Alzheimer's. The Alzheimer's Association explains that compared to people without diabetes, more people with diabetes get dementia. The forms of dementia are Alzheimer's disease and vascular dementia.

What is the diabetes-dementia link? Doctors don't know yet what causes Alzheimer's disease or exactly how diabetes and dementia are connected. Nevertheless, they do know that insulin resistance, high blood sugar or diabetes can harm the brain in several ways:

- Insulin resistance and Type 2 diabetes increase the risk of heart disease and stroke. These conditions hurt the heart and blood vessels. Damaged blood vessels in the brain may contribute to Alzheimer's disease.

- The brain depends on many different chemicals. Too much insulin may upset the balance of these chemicals. Some of these changes may help trigger Alzheimer's disease.

- High blood sugar causes inflammation. This may damage brain cells and help Alzheimer's to develop.

I think it would be beneficial to point out that, if using fish oil to keep you brain healthy works to prevent Alzheimer's disease then why not do it? I think a pleasant side effect would be that your OCD symptoms also improve. A healthy brain makes a happy brain.

There are other supplements, herbal ones, which I use to help with OCD symptoms. Bach, a good brand of natural remedies, carries a wonderful array of original flower essences that seem to help when you need that extra little boost. I tend to worry to excess about my loved ones. Their wellbeing is often one of my many repetitive thoughts. So I tried Bach's Red Chestnut. It says right on the label that it "allows you to love without anxiety or fear for the well-being of your loved ones". How cool is that? Directions for use are right on the label too.

I also use Mimilus, which "brings courage and calm to face things that frighten or worry you, also aids the shy and timid". I use Gentian, which "inspires a positive attitude when you feel discouraged or despondent due to setbacks", and it is an absolute must for me. Taking Cherry Plum "helps you act rationally and think clearly with a calm and balanced mind when you fear losing control". Lastly, I use White Chestnut that "encourages a peaceful and calm mind when thoughts and worries go round and round in your head". I think Dr. Edward Bach made these especially for those of us who live with OCD.

As with any supplement, always ask your doctor if you should use them. Also, you can check a very reliable source on the internet to see if these herbs/flower essences will not work well with you current medications, or if you should not be using them because of certain illnesses, or whether it's safe or not for you to use during pregnancy or breastfeeding. This resource is www.mountainroseherbs.com, you can look up the herbs/flower essences under products then herbs, and after finding the herb you're looking for, check its **contemporary info.** This is also a great website where I purchase many of my herbs to make certain tinctures and tonics.

A great book on using herbs that I recommend to all my family and friends is *Healing Tonics* by Jeanine Pollak. I use this book all the time for calming OCD symptoms. Not only does this book contain recipes for building your immunity or making lovely recipes for company, it also contains recipes for "If I only had a Brain" tea, "Brain Tonic" tincture, "Temperament Tonics", "Raging moods" calming nerve tea, "Spaz Away" tincture (personal favorite), "Kami's Garden" nerve tonic bath, "Knockout-Drops" relaxing tincture, and "Easy-Does-It" relaxing tea just to name a few. I love, love, love this book!

That pretty much sums up the diet portion of this chapter. Now, as far as exercise is concerned, everybody knows you should exercise at least 30 minutes three times a week. Whether it's walking, bicycling, yoga, swimming, or whatever, you should be doing it at least three times a week. Many people exercise for different reasons.

Someone may exercise to control their weight, another may exercise to control their diabetes or to help with cholesterol or any number of other bodily issues. No one really thinks to exercise for the mind or the brain. If you think about it, the brain is the most important part of the body that you should care for.

The Franklin Institute has published some very interesting stuff on the subject of exercise and the benefits of it on the human brain. Check it out at www.fi.edu/learn/brain/exercise. html#physicalexercise. Apparently, "walking is especially good for the brain, because it increases blood circulation and the oxygen and glucose that reach your brain." I suppose this would explain why my guardian angels suggested I go for lots of walks out in nature as mentioned in Chapter One. See? They knew the benefits.

The Franklin Institute also has other studies that show that walking can improve your memory. It would make sense, after all, more blood flow to the brain keeps the brain healthier, which makes you healthier and happier, which I believe is what we all strive for.

There are all sorts of information out there concerning this area of study. More and more people are realizing the effects on the brain of a good diet and plenty of exercise. In *Spark: The Revolutionary New Science of Exercise and the Brain*, John J. Ratey says that exercise pumps more oxygenated blood throughout your body, including the brain. This means that your brain gets "stronger". Not only does the brain strengthen, but Dr. Ratey also showed how exercise helps the brain to produce more Brain-Derived Neurotrophic Factor (BDNF). Apparently, this protein helps brain cells to grow and communicate between each other in a better way.

So not only does exercise reduce stress, but it also seems to improve the mind-body connection which is important when living with OCD. As proper diet can protect your brain from Alzheimer's and dementia and ease OCD, exercise does the same.

CHAPTER FOUR ~
Chakras and Color Therapy

I discovered chakras for myself during my meditation-learning phase. I never knew anything about chakras until I started meditating and reading up on the subject. I can just see some people rolling their eyes on this one, but believe it or not, I think chakras are a **very real** thing. The body and spirit are composed of energy, and at the root of every psychological problem is an energy problem. A great book that I found extremely helpful is *Chakra Therapy* by Keith Sherwood. His book goes into great detail concerning chakras and human psychology.

"The subtle energy system is composed of nadis which conduct Prana through the subtle bodies, the three auras (the reservoirs of energy surrounding the four bodies), the Hara, located three fingers below the navel (the fulcrum from which everything else is balanced), and the seven chakras." Keith Sherwood.

Chakra is a Sanskrit word that means "wheel", and are considered the energy centers of the body. They exist in the surface of the etheric double of man and are located on the spine and up into the head. The chakras connect the nadis, channels through which energy flows, with the three auras that surround the physical and the subtle/etheric bodies.

Chakras are like beautiful little rotating fans/vortices of subtle energy that pick up and transform energy entering the body into emotional and physical sensations, even thought. Thus, if a person is constantly bombarded with negative energy, psychological problems can arise or worsen if they already exist.

There are many chakras in the human body, but generally, the main seven that are located along the spine and up into the head are as follows:

> **Muladhara** ~ Base or Root Chakra (area of the coccyx governing ovaries/prostate, controls excretion, digestion of food, and health of small intestine, colon, and kidney)

> **Svadhisthana** ~ Sacral Chakra (located just above the sexual organs, regulates sexual energy such as intrinsic masculinity or femininity, and is the seat of creativity)

> **Manipura** ~ Solar Plexus Chakra (area of the navel, the seat of personality)

> **Anahata** ~ Heart Chakra (area of the heart, associated with healing and compassion)

> **Vishuddha** ~ Throat Chakra (throat and neck area, associated with the internal world, things ethereal, hearing, and sound)

> **Ajna** ~ Brow or Third Eye Chakra (associated with the pituitary gland, known as third eye, Ohm, Yin and Yang)

> **Sahasrara** ~ Crown Chakra (located at top of the head, corresponds with pineal gland, associated with achieving wholeness, merging the I AM with the ALL, highest level of spiritual perfection)

Each chakra is also associated with a color, generally following the colors of the spectrum (or the rainbow). The reason for this is not because it's just pretty, but because it is a fact that the entire spectrum of colors comes from white light, or sunlight. Each color in this electromagnetic spectrum/rainbow has its own wavelength and frequency. Colors actually affect us, and that is one of the reasons that chakras are associated with color.

The order of the chakra colors, starting with the base or first chakra is as the order of the spectrum/rainbow. The base or first chakra is red, second chakra is orange, third chakra is yellow, and so forth until arriving at the crown chakra which is violet when clear and activated.

For each chakra, there are specific meditations that you can do. Or as a beginner, you could do a complete meditation on all seven chakras at once. The point of the meditations is to clear the debris that any negativity has left behind on the chakras. This negativity can cause all sorts of problems energetically as well as physically. Clearing the chakras in turn clears your body and mind.

A good beginner meditation that I still use is a guided one by Doreen Virtue called *Chakra Cleansing*, which has both a morning and evening meditation. Each of these meditations takes about 20 minutes. Sometimes I find that if I'm in a hurry, and I don't quite feel "right", I take a moment and quiet myself by closing my eyes, breathing deeply a couple times, and then focusing on my chakras. Then very quickly, like flipping on a light switch, I work my way up from the base chakra to the crown chakra, and imagine that a little light comes on for each as I "flip the switch". In my mind, the light clears the chakras and activates them with loving energy. Then with a few more deep breathes I open my eyes and feel quite energized and ready to go on with whatever I was doing. If you require more of a "fix", after this quick little "flipping the switch" chakra imagery, you could try to imagine a white light shining brightly from each of the chakras, again starting at the base and working your way up, connecting each other with every breath you take. If you want to connect yourself even further with God or the universe, you can imagine a white light that has connected all the chakras moving up and through the top of your head, or the crown chakra, and shooting straight to the Divine. Feel yourself connecting, and then "cap off" the top of your head. As a beginner, you just need to see yourself filled with this divine light throughout the day to remind yourself that you are connected, that you are part of the universe and part of God.

Another way to work with chakras is to use color therapy. Color therapy, or chromo therapy, has been in use for millennia. There is evidence that it was used in ancient Egypt, Greece and China. If using the fact that light is composed of the spectrum/rainbow and that colors have their own wavelength and frequency, then one could surmise that like the chakras, our tissues and organs need that same healing energy from the light. "When disease or injury disturbs the vibration and energy of an organ or area of our body, applying the associated color frequency can restore the body to health. Eastern medical practice teaches that we have meridians that carry energy through the body and connect to each organ. Each color's vibration is associated with different attributes and qualities. The colors also can influence our emotions and well-being by supplying the frequency we need to keep our mind and body in balance. Color does not heal. Rather, it enables the body to heal itself." ~ www.therapycolor.com.

If you're interested in trying color therapy, an effective and convenient way to do this is by wearing **color therapy glasses.** "It is believed that the color entering the eyes is directed to the hypothalamus gland, from there to the pineal gland and then to the pituitary gland, which regulates and governs hormone production. As the brain processes this information, it is believed that it causes cellular and hormonal changes. The key is that the frequency of the color may be transmitted to the area of the body that recognizes it. The frequency, or vibration, of the color is constant. The vibration can "tune" that area of the body. In other words, that area may now be restored to its proper vibration and be restored to health while the color is being used. If used regularly, the body may learn to function properly on its own, much as it will with physical therapy." ~ www.color-medicine.com.

Another way to use color therapy is to use colored bulbs to bathe external problem areas on your body with the colored light. One quick thing that I like to do is to wear certain colored clothing for specific effects. For example, if I'm feeling down, wearing a bright shirt sometimes elevates my mood. I also have painted the rooms in my house certain specific colors. Feng Shui says certain colors are great only in certain rooms. For example, a bedroom is meant for sleep, so you wouldn't paint it a wild color. For my son's room, we chose blue, which is cooling, and green, which is calming. Both are great for bedrooms.

The following list gives color descriptions and a few of the healing effects. You can find the full lists at www.color-medicine.com. One interesting note; you might notice that these descriptions coincide with the chakra's descriptions given earlier in this chapter.

COLOR	BENEFIT
RED	Chronic pain - May lower the frequency of wavelengths causing them to be less excited and thereby reduce pain. Reduce migraine symptoms Stimulates the liver Helps with female disorders Increases heart strength and stimulates circulation Increases blood flow to the brain Provides seasickness relief
ORANGE	Stimulates the lungs and thyroid gland to increase oxygen to the body For lactating mothers, stimulates the mammary glands resulting in increased milk production for women who breastfeed their babies. Reduces menstrual cramps Relieves cramping, cramps and convulsions in all parts of the body Relieves digestive gas, flatulence Helps lungs and stimulates the respiratory system. Used to treat Chronic Obstructive Pulmonary Disease (COPD), Emphysema, Chronic Bronchitis, Asthma, and Tuberculosis.

COLOR	BENEFIT
YELLOW	Can help with night blindness because it filters out blue light Increases appetite, and tends to cause better assimilation of food for better nutrition Increases healing for all kinds of paralysis from stroke to sluggish organs, and stimulates and builds nerves Strengthens heart resulting in better circulation Improves rheumatoid arthritis, neuritis and similar conditions because yellow may help eliminate calcium and lime deposits
GREEN	Provides for overall wellbeing, for chronic or acute issues Facilitates healing of sores, bruises and cuts. Used for treatments of burns Stimulates the brain Stimulates the digestive system Increases dissolving of blood clots Reduces tremors, twitching, shaking
AQUA	Rebuilds the skin when damaged by burns, scratches, infections or sores. Relieves pain from burns. Helps with scaring. Fever relief Removes muscle fatigue toxins from the body. Relieve aches and pains. A mild sedative with no side effects Harmonizes all circulation processes Relieves headaches Macular degeneration: reported to improve vision and relieve stress on the eyes.

COLOR	BENEFIT
BLUE	Associated with the thyroid, parathyroid, throat, mouth and lungs. A few of the possible benefits: Acts as a bactericide. Useful in the treatment of acne and other skin disorders. Relaxes and calm muscles Helps with weight loss Slightly stronger than turquoise for the relief of burns and fevers Rebuilds the skin when damaged by burns, scratches, infections or sores Helps with dyslexia
INDIGO	May depress the thyroid while stimulating the parathyroid at the same time Use indigo for ear, eye, sinus, throat and nasal problems. An analgesic. Reduces swelling relieving the associated pain. A strong sedative resulting in a deep sleep. Upon awakening, you will feel rested, refreshed and alert.
VIOLET	Overall immune enhancer Stimulates hormonal activity. Use it on the throat to stimulate the thyroid For over excitable people, may relax and calm the nerves Depresses the appetite Deep, restful sleep
MAGENTA	Stimulates and builds up the heart Brings blood pressure within normal range, whether up or down Stimulates or depresses arteries or veins to bring them to normal Stimulates or depresses adrenal glands and kidneys to bring them to normal

COLOR	BENEFIT
BAKER-MILLER PINK	Appetite suppressant Relaxation Stress relief Calming aggression

The use of color to treat ailments is a fascinating idea. I've tried it and it seems to work. Simply changing my wardrobe to certain colors or decorating my house in specific hues has made a lot of difference. Again, different colored light bulbs can change the mood of a room, thus changing your mood. Perhaps this is where the term "looking through rose colored glasses" came from. It seems that looking through pink glasses would be very relaxing and calming, ideal for those of us with OCD.

CHAPTER FIVE ~

Reiki

Reiki is a very popular and fast growing form of energy healing. I myself have used it and got excellent results. Therefore, I am including it in this book as a form of living with OCD.

For those individuals who have not heard of Reiki, it is a non-invasive Japanese technique that promotes healing through relaxation and stress reduction. It is not a religion but a spiritual practice or way of life. It was developed in 1922 by Mikao Usui, a Japanese Buddhist. He believed that a peaceful and harmonious life was important, which is true for so many other cultures. But Mikao Usui's point was that Reiki healing wouldn't work unless both the healer and the person being healed were open to the healing. An interesting little tidbit, "the word Reiki is made of two Japanese words - Rei which means "God's Wisdom or the Higher Power" and Ki which is "life force energy". So Reiki is actually "spiritually guided life force energy."" ~ The International Center for Reiki Training (www.reiki.org).

The way Reiki works is based on the recognition that the body is or is filled with energy. The energy, or life force, flows through the body along chakras, nadis, meridians, and through our auras, which is the field of energy surrounding our bodies. As mentioned earlier, if this energy flow is blocked in some way, then our physical bodies can very easily feel the disruption. This disruption causes all sorts of mayhem, both in the physical body and the mind. This is where the use of Reiki healing can come in handy for those who live with OCD. Because OCD is so centered on thoughts and feelings, Reiki as a form of alternative treatment is very useful. When we are constantly bombarded with negative thoughts and feelings during our daily lives, sometimes this negative stuff "sticks" to us by attaching onto our energy field. This blockage is what causes loss of energy, or illness, depression and anxiety. All of which is a no-no for OCD people.

Most modern religions recognize some form of laying hands on a sick or injured person as a way to either ease suffering or facilitate healing. Perhaps the modern use of Reiki was a rediscovery of a very old and lost tradition, for Reiki healing is performed by laying on hands. Now the healer does not actually lay their hands on your body at any time. They hold their hands over the area that needs treatment and a flow of warm energy can literally be felt transferring through and around you, as well as back and forth between you and the healer.

I remember my first Reiki treatment very well. I went in for a healing, but didn't tell the Reiki healer the specifics, because I was still skeptical at that point. So we just decided to do a full body healing. So there I was, lying there very comfortably and very open to the possibility that something great would happen. She started at my head and from the very first minute she said, "Wow, there's a LOT of blockage here!" Perhaps she was sensing the OCD? She worked on it by holding her hands over my head for quite a while. There was a feeling of warmth, a kind of heat, radiating all around my head, inside and out. It was weird, but so beautiful at the same time. And as she worked down my body, she noted good things, like how I have a lot of heart energy. She also sensed and cleansed my body of blockages in my pelvic region. I had just had a miscarriage and surgery several months before this Reiki healing. I was trying to get pregnant again, with no success. She said it was because there was too much negative energy and I needed to work on clearing it. She showed me an exercise, which was very helpful. Basically,

I was to envision a bright light from above coming into my crown chakra, down through my body, scrubbing my pelvic region clean, and then shooting out through my toes and into the earth. It was very cleansing and very grounding.

After finishing my Reiki treatment, I remember her helping me off the table. I'll never forget this feeling because it felt like I was weightless! My feet felt like they were floating several feet off the floor and I could breathe so easily. How did I survive before this treatment? Not only did I feel warm and healed, but also peaceful and relaxed and just a general sense of healthy wellbeing. Plus, after working the exercises that she showed me, I conceived a couple months later.

This list of benefits from Reiki healing can be found at www. reiki-for-holistic-health.com. "When we are relaxed, stress-free, we are able to restore our natural ability to heal".

REIKI:

- Creates deep relaxation and assists the body to release stress and tension
- It accelerates the body's self-healing abilities
- Assists with improving sleep quality
- Reduces blood pressure
- Helps with acute (injuries) and chronic problems (asthma, eczema, headaches, etc.) and assists the breaking of addictions
- Helps relieve pain
- Removes energy blockages, adjusts the energy flow of the endocrine system bringing the body into balance and harmony
- Assists the body in cleaning itself from toxins
- Reduces some of the side effects of drugs and helps the body to recover from drug therapy after surgery

- Supports the immune system
- Increases vitality and postpones the aging process
- Raises the vibrational frequency of the body
- Helps spiritual growth and emotional clearing

So Reiki as a treatment for OCD could be very beneficial, especially if done on a long-term basis with a well-qualified Reiki healer.

CHAPTER SIX ~

Facing Your Fear

Facing your fear...yikes! This is always a difficult subject to approach. Everyone has different fears. Some fears are based on something dangerous, like a fear of falling from heights. Other fears are miniscule in comparison, but just as debilitating for someone with OCD, such as a fear of mice. In this chapter, we discuss a specific OCD treatment that worked for me, Exposure and Response Prevention. With this type of treatment, one can get over their fear of heights or their fear of mice.

In the medical community, it is very well known that one of the most effective treatments for OCD is that of Cognitive-behavioral therapy, which consists of cognitive therapy and exposure/response prevention.

"The **cognitive therapy** component for obsessive-compulsive disorder (OCD) focuses on the catastrophic thoughts and exaggerated sense of responsibility you feel. A big part of cognitive therapy for OCD is teaching you healthy and effective ways of responding to obsessive thoughts, without resorting to compulsive behavior." www.helpguide.org.

"**Exposure and response prevention** involves repeated exposure to the source of your obsession. Then you are asked to refrain from the compulsive behavior you'd usually perform to reduce your anxiety." www.helpguide.org.

Let's use me as an example. I am a compulsive hand washer. Therefore, an exposure and response technique that worked for me was to pet and play with my dogs and then refrain from washing my hands. With this exercise, "as you sit with the anxiety, the urge to wash your hands will gradually begin to go away on its own. In this way, you learn that you don't need the ritual to get rid of your anxiety – that you have some control over your obsessive thoughts and compulsive behaviors" www.helpguide.org. Unbelievably, it did work. But again, like with so many other OCD symptoms, stress can make things worse or return. So if you are able to get rid of a certain OCD symptom but in the future it returns due to a stressful situation in your life, don't be hard on yourself. Lapses happen, it's ok. Just remember how you got rid of it the first time, and do it again. It works every time.

There are books and studies that show exposure and response prevention can actually "retrain" the brain so that the OCD symptoms will eventually go away. One such book that I found immensely helpful and insightful was *Change You Brain, Change Your Life* by Daniel G. Amen, M.D. published in 1998. You may have heard of this book, it was on the New York Times Bestseller.

One way of exposure therapy to work is to get your family members involved. My sister seems to be very understanding of my OCD. She and my husband try to accommodate me and I appreciate it, but I wonder sometimes if this "cooperation" could be hurtful more than helpful. For example, my son and I visited my sister and her husband for a week in 2005. At that point in time I was off of my medication trying to see if I could survive un-medicated life with OCD. It wasn't really working, because I didn't have the right coping tools to help me.

I was really afraid of many things, including colors. Certain colors, like red and brown, just gave me the shivers. If I saw, came near, or was forced to touch one of these colors, I would completely lose it. It's bizarre that I was afraid of the color brown, because I have brown hair, brown eyes, and my favorite food, chocolate, is brown!

But I didn't own brown clothes, brown shoes, or anything else that was brown.

I suppose my fear of the color brown more related to the word than to the actual color. I knew someone named Brown who had a serious illness, so I guess the word and color usually reminded me of this person. In my own OCD way of thinking, I guess I thought that brown would somehow contaminate me. I knew that this was completely ridiculous, yet it still took control of my life. This way of thinking is indeed "nonsense", but that's how the OCD brain works.

I had to keep reminding myself that brown is just a color, a good color, and it could not hurt me. I knew this, yet it still bothered me. I was getting the "cognitive" part of the solution, but was totally missing the exposure/response portion of the situation. No matter how much I kept telling myself that "it was safe and ok", I still wouldn't touch anything brown or buy brown clothes, etc. It is so frustrating how debilitating OCD can be at times.

So let's go back to the story. We were at my sister's house getting ready for bed and low and behold, she pulls out brand new **brown** bed sheets, which she bought just for us. I had a lump in my throat, my heart started racing, and I went pale. She asked me "what's wrong?" So I told her of my phobia and regrettably, she had no other clean sheets. Therefore, it was either the brown sheets, or the bare mattress on the old pullout sofa. Well, I was embarrassed, so I chose the sheets. My sister apologized profusely, but it wasn't her fault. Brown is her favorite color, and she had it everywhere. This was my problem, not hers. So I knew this was something I would just have to overcome, right then and there!

As you probably already know, people with OCD can fall into several categories. There is the "checker" who is constantly making sure that things are turned off and doors are locked, the "washer" who is almost always washing something whether it's dirty or not because of possible contamination, the "arrangers/counters" who make sure everything is in order and even, the "hoarders" which keep everything because something might be needed in the future, and my personal favorite (not really) the "sinners/doubters" who think that if they have a "bad" thought or don't do something just right, that something bad will happen. I'm one of the few who fall into every single category.

My problem with the color brown fell into the "washer" and "sinners/doubters" category. I thought that if I touched the color brown that something bad would happen to us. I crawled into bed after praying to God to protect me and my son, whom was sleeping next to me, from whatever the "something bad" would possibly be. With all of these worries, I was convinced I would be up all night obsessing, but to my relief, I fell asleep very quickly. I suppose I was tired from traveling and all the accompanying stress. The next morning I awoke and much to my surprise, I thought, "I survived!" So for a whole week I slept in brown sheets! That is exposure/response therapy at work.

That whole experience for me was a blessing in disguise. You see, while my son and I were in Florida, my husband was in Pennsylvania looking for a place for us to rent. Apparently, there wasn't much to choose from, but he was able to find one place. The day my son and I arrived in Pennsylvania, my husband took us to the new house. To my horrific shock, the inside was completely brown; the walls, the floor, the carpet, the doors. Even the bathroom sink, tub, and toilet were brown. I was so depressed, but after a few days of being in there, cleaning, unpacking, and setting things up, I got used to it. After a few months, I fell in love with the place. And as far as the color brown is concerned, I use it all the time now. In clothing, shoes, purses, fabric, furnishings, and so on. With a smile on my face, I can say that I healed myself. The same can be true for you.

The fear of a color may seem silly and nonsensical, but it is still a fear nevertheless. And conquering that fear was a huge step in my healing process. As I said in the beginning of this chapter, some fears are big and some are small. Start with the small fears. Eventually you'll move on to the big fears. Now just remember to do no harm. Conquering fears is a mental game and should in no way harm you or anyone else in the process.

Remember the fear of the mouse? One way to conquer that would be simply to hold one. Remember the fear of falling from heights? I would not recommend facing that one. Maybe you could start small with a fear of falling from heights by standing on a small stepladder. Again, use common sense and do no harm to yourself or others.

Here is another example of OCD and facing your fears. When my husband first brought our son and me to our previously mentioned newly rented "brown" house in Pennsylvania, I saw that it was right next to a forest. Here it was, December and the trees were naked. I thought, "Cool, I really like trees and privacy". I got used to it while I attended college in Vermont. That's where my husband and I met, fell in love, and got married. Anyway, the only thing I really noticed those first couple of days at the new house was the fact that the interior was completely brown, like I said before. But soon I noticed something else. The trees outside "clacked" in the wind; and for some reason, I didn't like it. I found the clacking sound to be kind of creepy, especially when I was out alone at night looking at the stars through my telescope.

Another factor that added to the creepiness of the new place was the two rooms in the basement. I didn't like to go near them because not only were they very dark, but the antique doorknobs were covered in old chipped red paint. Red, as I mentioned before, was another problem color for me (which I have since also gotten over). When I first saw the two rooms in the basement, I immediately thought of that "Blair Witch" movie. The trees clacking outside reminded me of that, as well.

I didn't want to say anything. I thought I would just get over it. However, a couple weeks went by and I was still agitated. I decided to tell my husband about my annoying fears and how the creepy movie kept popping into my mind. "I knew you were going to say that!" he blurted out with a chuckle. "Really?" I asked. Then I thought about it. How did he know that I was thinking all of this, unless he was thinking it as well? This was an epiphany moment for me. My husband had the same thought! But why wasn't he obsessing about it like I was? That's the difference between an OCD brain and everyone else. We both thought the same thing, but my husband was able to let it go. My OCD brain couldn't. So there I was faced with the prospect of having to live with this creepiness or to face it and get over it. I chose to face it.

One thing that I did was to stay out longer at night when I was stargazing. I also turned my back to the woods and resisted the temptation to turn every time I heard a noise. I also reminded myself that there was nothing evil in the woods, the movie made me think that. I should not let creepy stories scare me. I also told myself that God made all of this beautiful land, the woods are peaceful and wonderful, and that clacking is just Mother Nature's wind chimes. It's music!

It took a few weeks, but I eventually started to really enjoy the woods. I even started walking through them by myself. I found the woods to be very beautiful, quiet, and peaceful when they're covered in snow. Sometimes I would sit there and think about things and eventually, the woods became my favorite place. It was like God's Cathedral, the woods. I loved it. Now, I find I do my best thinking outdoors and problems become solved with such clarity. Thank you God for the beautiful trees, clacking and all!

The whole point is to get better and live life to the fullest. If you can honestly say that you're living life to the fullest then you don't need this book. If you're not living life to the fullest and want to get better, just try a few of these techniques. I can say that for me, all of these have helped me one way or another. I feel my life improving every day, and it's exciting! Facing your fear can be hard, but the rewards far out-way the keeping of unhealthy OCD habits. Just give it a try; you'll see.

CHAPTER SEVEN ~

Past Life Regression

This in particular is a touchy subject. For one thing, the Christian religion does not believe in past lives, and another thing is most people just think it's silly. But with an open mind and an open heart, past life regression can heal in so many ways.

My first experience with past life regression was with Denise Linn in Orlando, Florida. It was at the 2006 "I Can Do It" conference and a couple hundred people surrounded me. I had never had a past life regression and was curious as well as doubtful. But I was at this conference to improve myself so I figured I should be open to it because maybe this is a piece of the healing puzzle.

The lecture started out with a story of her life, which was very fascinating, and then we went right into it. We broke up into groups of six with people that were immediately in our vicinity. She said it was no accident who we were sitting next to, that we were all connected in a past life somehow. I was getting really excited and nervous at the same time.

Denise Linn had the lights turned down very low, and then two performers, one being Dean Evenson, began playing the most beautiful music. Denise then guided us into a deep relaxation and we started our journey into a past life. It wasn't hypnosis, I was very aware of what was going on around me. It was just a deep relaxation and a sense of floating overcame me. I felt like I was deep inside my mind ready to explore.

Denise then guided us through a regression and I found myself walking in a little village. It was foggy and the grass was wet, and I looked down and realized that I was a young woman dressed in 17th century clothing. I remember resisting, but then deciding to just let it go and run with it. See where it took me. So I was walking in this village, and very quickly entered a little cottage. Inside I found myself with an older woman, not my mother or any relation. She felt to me to be more like my teacher. And then the weirdest thing happened. As I stood next to this woman, I realized that she was one of the women in our regression group of six. I was flabbergasted! Again, I had to remind myself just to go with it. So I looked around the cottage, which was basically one room with a large fireplace. We were standing at a table and she was showing me how to cook something. All sorts of herbs and roots and vegetables surrounded us. Moreover, I remember feeling very happy, but nervous at the same time.

The scene quickly changed to me being surrounded by a mob, and they were very angry and nasty. I felt like I couldn't move, I looked down, and realized that I was tied to a stake and they were burning me alive! To my horror, I realized what was going on... they were burning me as a witch! At this point, I think I threw in the towel to this whole past life regression thing. "Burned as witch, how utterly ridiculous" I thought to myself. "I've been watching too many movies." Not only that, but I had a deep fear of witches. I hated everything about them, I even hated Halloween. Nevertheless, I stuck with it and followed through the regression.

When we were finished, we were supposed to share our experiences with each other. To be honest, I don't really remember what the others said about their experiences. The whole time I was thinking, "Should I share what I experienced? Will they laugh at me? Was it real or did I make it up? Why did I see myself as a witch? I thought they were evil. I'm not evil!" All of a sudden, it was my turn. I took a deep breath and decided to share what I saw. I told them up front I wasn't sure if I believed it or not, but that I would have to decide that later for myself. To my surprise, almost everyone in the group believed the possibility of what I saw. I then told them how I saw the one other woman in our group there with me. She didn't seem surprised one bit. She then chimed in with a comforting smile "I was a teacher, and I know we shared a past life together. We were misunderstood and believed to be witches, and there were many of us that were hunted, burned and murdered at witch trials around the world."

I was speechless. I wasn't very familiar with witch trials. Growing up, I had only heard about the Salem witch trials. I didn't realize it happened all over the world. I made a mental note to do some research when I returned home.

The lecture/class was not finished. We were instructed to perform another exercise where the whole group closed their eyes and faced one person out of the group one at a time. We were to focus completely on that one person and then we each had a chance to tell what we saw about that person. This was very exciting because everyone in the group got results that were true and accurate. It's funny, because I don't remember what anyone said about me, but I remember what I said about everyone else. There was one woman who I saw dressed in a glorious gown singing on stage and she was just breathtakingly wonderful. It turns out she's an opera singer. I saw another man carving a wooden sculpture; he turned out to be an artist. I also saw another woman sitting at a loom weaving a beautiful cloth. Her response was that she had seen that before in previous regressions. I was just simply amazed at the whole experience.

So what's the point of all of this? Well, Denise Linn and others who believe in past life regression, believe that healings can occur during the process. Whether it's real or not, whether you believe or not, healings can occur. When the whole lecture was over, Denise reminded us to drink plenty of water and to not worry if there was a lingering stinky odor coming from us for the next two or three days. She said if that happened, all it meant was that we purged a lot of bad stuff and we were being cleansed, and possibly healed at the same time. I did indeed notice a strange odor and didn't make the connection until a day later when I remembered what Denise Linn had said about possibly experiencing this particular side effect. This made me think. Was it real?

On a side note, after this experience, I did some research on the witch trials when I returned home. Apparently, witch-hunts and trials did take place all over Europe for nearly three hundred years resulting in an estimated 100,000 deaths. I couldn't believe it. Was what I saw real? Was that possible? And what of the "healing" and the stinky odor that followed me around for two days? Well, surprisingly enough, my fear of fire is no longer a serious OCD issue for me. I remember from childhood up until this past life regression always having to check the stove to make sure it was off, planning exits in case of a fire, checking where the nearest exit was everywhere I went. I was so afraid of being trapped and burned. Now, I can actually leave the house without having to check the stove 10 times, or I can go out and not worry about being trapped and burned alive because every place you go already has an exit plan. I don't need to worry, just live! Needless to say, after having the time to do a little research on what I experienced, I am a true believer of past life regression and its healing abilities. It definitely worked for me. An extra perk; witches no longer scare me. I even dress up as a witch for Halloween.

In 2010 I had another major breakthrough with past life regression. Again it was with Denise Linn, this time in Toronto. In my regression, I saw myself as a young blonde woman walking on a mountain top road in the dark. It was a curvy dirt road and I realized that a car was coming up very quickly behind me. It was a very old car, perhaps one of the first models and it looked like the headlights were very dark. I didn't have room to jump out of the way, for the side of the road was on a cliff. The car swerved and went over the cliff. The man inside died. I then saw myself 10 or 15 years later and I was lying in bed dying and praying for forgiveness because I had blamed myself for that man's death all those years ago.

When we came out of the regression, I could not stop the tears from flowing. It was a cathartic cry and I was so surprised by this. I didn't cry when I saw myself burned alive at a stake, but I cried over this particular regression. It was slightly disturbing, but at the same time, I felt so much lighter like a weight had been lifted off of me. Sure enough, a stinky odor followed me for three days. So what was the healing that occurred, you may ask? Well, with my OCD issues, I used to blame myself for everything. It was very annoying for me and for my family. Everything that went wrong, with us or even around the world was somehow my fault. Either because I was being "punished" for something I had done and believed to be wrong, or because somehow through my thoughts I created whatever went wrong. Of course looking back, I realize how ridiculous all of that sounds, but when you have OCD, the ridiculous is the norm. The OCD brain is very intricate and maze-like. Once a thought is stuck in your head, you can be lost for hours, or in my case years.

I no longer feel the urge to blame myself for everything that goes wrong. I also realize that God is not a punishing God, He is a loving God. Every now and then, through stressful times, I may slip back to the blaming game, but it is so rare now that I can't really even remember the last time it happened. What a relief to go out into the world and to just enjoy it!

I love going to these conferences because I meet wonderful people and make new friends, but also because I have such growing knowledge coming from it all. If you would like to try past life regression, I recommend Denise Linn's cd *Journeys into Past Lives* and Doreen Virtue's cd *Past-Life Regression with the Angels*. They are both great introductions to past life regression and are also guided so you're not left alone, so to speak.

Healings can really occur from past life regressions. Now again, whether you believe it or not doesn't matter, the healing is still there. Just remember to have an open mind and an open heart. Go with the flow, you might surprise yourself. So go ahead and try it.

CHAPTER EIGHT ~

Thoughts Are Power

This chapter may be disturbing at first for some individuals with OCD, but I'm hoping by the end of it, things will seem clearer. The "thought" is the basis of most OCD problems. You see, the title of this chapter is "Thoughts Are Power", and this is so true. If you have OCD, I'm very sure your therapist has told you the standard quote that "Thoughts are just thoughts, they mean nothing". And although this helps those nasty thoughts seem less terrible and horrible, it's just a bandage. It doesn't actually "heal" the situation.

I've had an epiphany in the past year that has led to the writing of this book. That is that thoughts are not just thoughts, thoughts are everything! If you have OCD and have issues with "bad thoughts", I can imagine your heart skipping a beat and your stomach tightening right about now. Please bear with me, I am not trying to hurt you, I just want you to look at it from a different angle.

So here it is. Over the years of going to therapy for OCD and at the same listening to lectures and reading books about angels and spiritual life, I had come to realize how conflicting each of these was to the other. Completely opposite practically! But it took me a couple of years to whole-heartedly go from one side to the other and stay there. You see, in learning spiritual practices you constantly are told that thoughts are the most powerful thing in the universe. You can create with thoughts, and you can hurt with thoughts.

For example, you may be lonely and looking for love. You imagine the perfect mate, and then in one swift swoop you say how impossible it is ever to meet your perfect mate. You tell yourself how horribly lonely you will always be. Well, guess what? Those are the exact thoughts that keep you lonely. Instead, after imagining your perfect mate, tell yourself you are truly loved by God, tell yourself you are loved by your angels and ask them to help you find your mate because they do exist. Moreover, keeping these positive thoughts, or "happy thoughts" as I like to call them, will keep your heart open and attract this perfect mate into your life. It's amazingly true!

Now for the "bad thoughts" that some OCD people have; instead of saying that they're just thoughts and they mean nothing, try this approach. Cancel out the bad thought! I learned this canceling trick from Doreen Virtue. Just state it to the universe, aloud if you have to, that you cancel that bad thought in every and all directions of space and time and ask God (or the light) to cleanse you of this thought. Once the bad thought is canceled, you can also cancel the effects of that bad thought in every and all directions of space and time. After that, if the thought returns, which it most likely will, it doesn't matter if it does because it's already been canceled. I know this probably doesn't make sense, but it really works. You see, now that the bad thought has been canceled, I've discovered that you can replace it with a prayer or another "happy thought". Imagine and see the good thoughts in place of the bad thought that has already been canceled. It fixes everything and it's so delightfully simple.

The only trick if you have OCD and issues with repetitive habits is that you cannot let this become your new ritual. If the annoying thought returns just remind yourself that it's been canceled and then continue with one of the many relaxation techniques that we discussed in the previous chapters. Taking a deep breath always helps me. Alternatively, close your eyes and do a quick chakra cleanse. You could even try a full body relaxation exercise if you have the time. Even a change of scenery can help. I like to go outside, or if I can't, at least go to a different room or even change whatever activity I was doing at the time.

A couple years ago, I saw a great DVD about this very subject, which may help with this new way of thinking. It is called *The Secret* and has been out for quite a long time. Check it out; it may help with your journey of self-discovery and get you back on track to using your thoughts in a better way. It certainly instilled what I had already been thinking about to begin with; thoughts are power in a good way. It's quite amazing.

Just remember, God and your angels love you! Call on them if you ever need help. I've learned to control my "bad" thoughts for the most part, and hopefully this might work for you too.

CHAPTER NINE ~

Laughter

Whoever said laughter is the best medicine knew exactly what they were talking about. Not only is it the best medicine, but it is so much more fun than sitting there obsessing! Take my word for it. Cracking up with chuckles is so much more preferable than obsessing all day long. One quick thing that I did many years ago to get me out of my severe depression was to stop watching the news. I also stopped watching sad movies and certain dramas.

I know, you're probably thinking that I've got my head in the sand, but it really is a quick fix for a person with depression. Instead of all the sad stuff, watch comedies, read funny comics, read self-help books. That's what I did. It's been years since I started this lifestyle of keeping non-depressing stuff around me, and I like it that way. Who needs all those negative vibes constantly bombarding them? That stuff sticks around, remember the chapter on chakras?

My husband knows me pretty well, so he'll watch a movie sometimes and then tell me if I can handle it or not. In addition, as for the news, I noticed that if it's really important, I'd hear about it from friends or family. I don't need to sit there and watch those news programs that repeat twenty times in one hour all the horrible stuff that's happening.

I think the average person likes the sensationalism of the bad stuff. Maybe it's exciting to them. But to those of us who are sensitive, it's just very mind numbing and literally depressing. Many don't understand why I would "hide" from the negativity, but it's the lifestyle that I've chosen and it seems to be working for me. I don't necessarily consider it hiding, but more along the lines of shielding. It also makes it less horrible if when you do hear something tragic to just say a quick prayer and let it go.

One thing I'd like to mention here is that keeping track of the news, clinging to depressing situations, or even allowing depressing people to take over your lives can really bring you down. I'm talking literally lower your vibrational energy. Have you ever been in a room and then you could just "feel" another person coming in? You know by the feeling you get who it is. Test yourself one day either at work, or at even your own house. Keep your glance away from the door and just "feel" who's coming in. Nine times out of ten, you'll make the right guess.

So what is this vibrational energy? Many call this an aura. Whether you believe in them or not, is not the issue. The issue is that you can actually feel the energy or frequency that another person is living on. If the person is happy, their frequency of energy is higher and lighter. If the person is perpetually sad, their frequency is lower and denser. You can really feel this difference. That is why, when my depressions kicked in, I kept away from this lower energy, and tried to surround myself with a higher energy.

That's where laughter comes into the picture. I love to laugh. I love smiling too. In fact, I've been told several times how I'm always smiling or whistling happily. Smiles and laughter are really contagious too. I've noticed that when I smile or laugh, others do as well. I know I can't help but start laughing when I hear other people laughing. That's true for almost everyone.

The nice thing about laughter is that even if you're not a laughing kind of individual, you can learn to laugh. Even a fake laugh has been shown to improve your health. Apparently, there is a new type of yoga called Hasya Yoga, or laughter yoga that is gaining strong popularity. It comprises mostly of light breathing exercises, visualizations, and of course fake laughter. This fake laughter eventually grows into a real laughter that is, as mentioned earlier, very beneficial to one's health.

On March 19, 2005, the *Science Daily* did a report on a study done by the University of Maryland USA. This study conducted by researchers at the university concluded that the benefits of laughter were very much the same as the benefits gained during aerobic exercise. These benefits include a release of endorphins, which are natural painkillers, an increase in blood flow, boosts in the immune system, and of course the reduction of any stress and anxiety that one may be experiencing at the time. The study also confirmed previous studies that suggested a link between mental stress and the narrowing of blood vessels. That right there is exactly what I've been talking about. Laughter can heal!

I remember as a teenager going to a funeral of a young co-worker who had been killed in a car wreck. I cried for days and all through the funeral. However, on the way home from the funeral, I was carpooling with other co-workers and someone just started giggling. And before long, we were all chuckling. I don't know why, we just were. I said I felt guilty for giggling, especially since the funeral only ended a short while ago. My friend who was driving said, "It doesn't mean we won't remember her, but our lives must go on. It's ok to laugh. It's ok to feel better. Be glad you're alive."

Therefore, laughter really is the best medicine. What if you're not big into laughing? Well, start out by just smiling. Pretty soon, others will be smiling right back at you. Remember what I mentioned earlier; keep comedy in your life. Remove the negative and keep the positive, and pretty soon you'll be laughing all the time, even at yourself!

CHAPTER 10 ~

Gratitude

Gratitude is something that I'm sure you've heard of. People talk about it a lot lately. But gratitude is such a little miracle in itself and it is such a good way to heal oneself. It's simple really; just start making an effort to be grateful.

Someone once told me a very long time ago, that I was not a gracious or grateful person. I was shocked, but that statement made me take a long hard look at myself. And you know what? They were right. Only my OCD made me take this newly found realization to the extreme. I started thinking that my thoughts and actions were hurting people, all people, everywhere. I didn't understand why there are bad things in the world that happened to people. I became afraid of everything and everyone, because I was scared of being hurt or others being hurt because of me. The realization that I couldn't control everything on the planet didn't hit me until years later. The stress in my life was horrible because of all the blame I piled onto myself. Gratitude and its simple beauty would've saved me many restless days and nights at that time in my life. I didn't find the balance of graciousness and gratitude, until years later when my son was born.

With my newly born son in my life, I learned the power of gratitude. Simply be thankful. And I was. I was so thankful; thankful for my little baby, thankful for my wonderful husband, and thankful for everything in my life. I started making lists of things of which I was grateful for. You can be grateful for anything; whatever pops into your heart or your mind.

If you're new to this, start small. You can be grateful for your body, your hands and feet, eyes and ears, your beautiful mind. You can be grateful for the air you breathe, for the beautiful flowers in your garden, or for the beautiful moonlight shining through your window. You can be grateful for your loved ones, their good health, and the good things we have in our lives that most people take for granted. Such as clean food and water, the roof over your head, or even the fact that we live in a time with toilets! After some time, you may even become grateful for all the trials and hardships you may have experienced in the past because you know they happened for a reason. For me, I wouldn't be the person I am today without everything that happened to me. And I love me, I love who I am. Therefore, I am grateful for my past whether it was easy or not.

I am reminded of one of my favorite childhood movies *Pollyanna*. She used to play the "glad game" whenever things didn't go right for her, and I think I've always carried that memory with me. The glad game is gratitude, and I've been playing it for years now.

The nice thing is, that with gratitude comes forgiveness. I've noticed that I found myself letting go of old grudges and old hurt feelings. Forgiveness, whether you forgive the individual or situation in person or in the privacy of your own mind, is cleansing. With this cleansing and newfound gratitude for absolutely everything comes the healing. I started to see my life improve in leaps and bounds. Especially with the arrival of my long awaited daughter being born into our lives.

I suppose another miracle from all of this gratefulness and forgiving, is that I started seeing life in a completely new light. Everything is beautiful, everyone is beautiful, and you can see it. You can see God in everything. And best of all, my relationship with God and all that is in the Light, is getting better every day. What a magnificent spiritual journey I have been on. I know that what is to come will be even more wonderful and thrilling and I can honestly say that I am ready.

I only hope and pray that what I have written here will help you. Like I said before, I'm not a doctor or an expert, I just lived through it is all. Please, please go see a doctor if the OCD is really bad. There's nothing wrong with getting help. I only wanted to show that there are alternative methods you can use to accompany your treatments. Once you get better and if the doctor lets you go, like mine set me free, then you can decide what's good for you and your way of life. I pray for your healing to be swift and your journey of self-discovery to be wonderful. May the blessings of God and His Light shine upon you always. Amen. Much love to you all.